HandsOn
NASHVILLE

Celebrating its 20th anniversary, Hands On Nashville is Middle Tennessee's volunteer resource center and one of the largest nonprofits of its kind in the United States. In 2010, HON connected nearly 200,000 volunteers with service opportunities, which included a historic volunteer mobilization in response to the May 2010 flood. HON volunteers work 365 days each year to support 25 critical community needs, ranging from hunger and homelessness to at-risk youth and animal welfare. For more information or to volunteer, visit www.hon.org or call (615) 298-1108.

All proceeds from the sale of "Take My Hand" support HON in its mission to connect volunteers with community need.

- *Mayor Dean volunteers at a water distribution site.* -

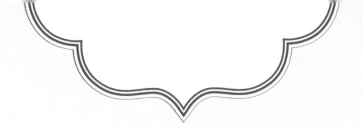

FOREWORD

~ *By* Mayor Karl Dean ~

This book celebrates the thousands of Nashvillians who refused to let tragedy bring our city down, and an organization that bound those people together. It is about the volunteers who worked night and day to help total strangers, and about Hands On Nashville, the organization that led the volunteer effort.

A series of events on Monday, May 3, 2010, the day the Cumberland River crested after two days of heavy rain, sticks in my mind as a great demonstration of the effectiveness of Hands On Nashville. I was in the emergency headquarters around mid-morning, as was Hands On Nashville Director Brian Williams. Concerns about the rising waters near downtown were growing, and Brian said he would see what volunteers could do to help.

By 2:30 that afternoon, Hands On Nashville had already recruited 150 volunteers to the threatened area at MetroCenter, and they formed an assembly line that moved hundreds of 50-pound sandbags into position to save the area from flooding. Those bags are very heavy, and the weather that day was like a steam bath.

It was a tremendous demonstration of the organization's effectiveness and the dedication of those volunteers.

As I walked through flood-ravaged neighborhoods, I was also impressed by the way volunteers had helped clean our city up and move it forward. I have seen volunteer efforts elsewhere in which volunteers show up and have little to do. The experience leaves them disgruntled. But Hands On Nashville did a great job of matching people with work in a way that allowed everyone to contribute.

As for the volunteers and the way they turned out in huge numbers to help others, I cannot say enough about their importance during this disaster. Church groups, civic organizations, employers, even jail inmates gave freely of themselves and their time to help others. I can say that it was an incredible testimony to the people of Nashville.

I travel to other cities and people stop me to say that they heard about the way people reacted in Nashville during the flood and the way we all came together. It makes you feel very proud that our city is recognized that way. Even people who couldn't physically contribute to the cleanup effort helped in other ways, such as voluntarily cutting their water usage.

Thanks to every one of the volunteers who took part in that effort. This book is a celebration of your great work.

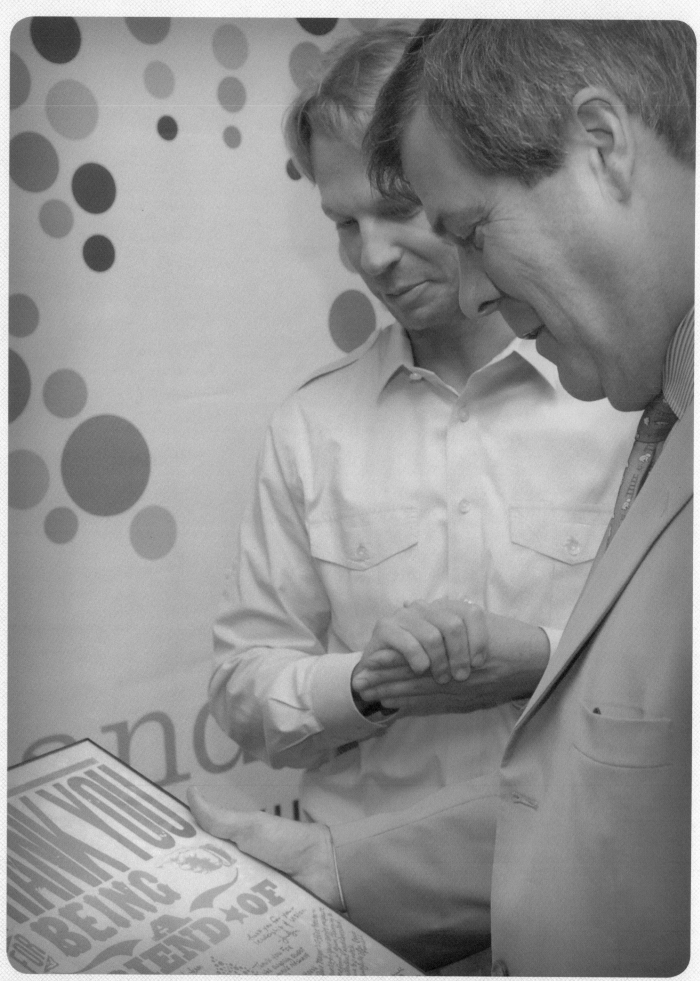

- *Brian presents a Hatch Show Print to Mayor Dean to thank him for his leadership.* -

INTRODUCTION

By Brian N. Williams, HON Executive Director

As Middle Tennessee's volunteer resource center, Hands On Nashville knows that service can be transformative. In our agency's 20-year history, volunteers' contributions were never more widespread, tangible and life-changing than in the wake of the May 2010 flood.

On May 1 and 2, approximately 13 inches of rain fell, leading to a 1,000-year flood that devastated West and Middle Tennessee. The Cumberland River crested in Nashville at nearly 52 feet, 12 feet above flood stage. When the rain stopped, Nashville-Davidson County and 47 other Tennessee counties were declared federal disaster areas. Nineteen people were killed. An estimated $3 billion in damage was sustained.

The response was extraordinary. Few could have imagined how Nashville, or any community, might have faced a natural disaster of this enormity with more dignity, courage and generosity. All Middle Tennesseans were affected, either personally or through friends' and family members' hardships. Yet everyone banded together to help others. From Mayor Karl Dean and Metro Council members to celebrities like Ke$ha and Kerry Collins, volunteers from around the corner and around the globe offered their hands and rose to the challenge.

Between May 3 and December 31, more than 22,000 people donated 91,000 hours to flood recovery and restoration efforts in more than 1,200 volunteer projects through Hands On Nashville alone. To put 91,000 hours into perspective, that's nearly 11 years of time.

The economic value of these volunteers' human capital exceeded $2 million.

Yet, the sum impact of service is far greater. The previously mentioned numbers account only for the verified service contributed by volunteers registered through www.hon.org. They do not include the more than 100,000 volunteer referrals made by Hands On Nashville to facilitate grassroots efforts led by individuals, as well as faith and community groups, in 2010. Nor do they reflect the countless hours contributed through other organizations or volunteers who just showed up and started working.

To commemorate this historic volunteer response a year later, Hands On Nashville offers "Take My Hand: How Nashville United In The Wake Of The 2010 Flood." Its 20 stories share a sampling of the remarkable work volunteers did and continue doing today to provide flood relief to those in need. There are thousands more stories, reminding us that ordinary people accomplish extraordinary things. "Take My Hand" celebrates each of your contributions to volunteerism.

May 2011 also marks the 20th anniversary of Hands On Nashville, an agency that exists because of thousands of people who share their time, talent and treasure to give others a hand up.

To all of you who have volunteered through nonprofits, schools, government agencies, faith-based organizations, civic groups and businesses over the last 20 years: Thank you. You are heroes.

Let's start our next 20 years together by volunteering and being the change we want to see in our community and our world. Our time is now. Together, let's create 200,000 more remarkable volunteer stories.

CONTENTS

Photos of volunteers' hands by Michael Krouskop.

NASHVILLE CAMARADERIE

Freelance photographer Nate Johnson set out for MetroCenter on May 3 to take photos of volunteers stacking sandbags in a battle against the rising floodwaters of the nearby Cumberland River. They would make a good addition to his professional portfolio, he thought.

A few hours later, after viewing through his camera lens the camaraderie of hundreds of Hands On Nashville volunteers, he was inspired to become part of the picture as a laborer instead of a photographer.

Nate joined the volunteers as they formed assembly lines to transfer hundreds of sandbags up a hill and stack them in a 5-foot-high wall to protect the business park in case of a levee collapse.

He described what he called the coolest moment of the day as when he climbed up to the interstate and took a bird's-eye picture of the volunteers. "It was a massive amount of people," he said. "That's when it clicked in my mind that this was an amazing group effort."

In addition to helping on the sandbagging line, Nate was present, either as a volunteer or as a photographer, at three other Hands On Nashville flood relief projects. As a volunteer, he was assigned to a neighborhood block near a water plant and walked from house to house asking families if they needed help with anything. For one elderly couple in the process of relocating, he helped take out what was being thrown away, bag up what they were keeping and lay out photos that needed to dry.

"I definitely feel part of the community here. My greatest friends are here, I don't know that I'll always stay here, but I know I'll always be part of the people here."

Nate also helped document the citywide effort, taking photos at two Hands On Nashville water distribution points near the Nashville Fairgrounds, where volunteers directed cars and handed out bottles of water to people as they approached the site.

{ "The morale of the volunteers was almost too good to be true," Nate said. "It was this common purpose. No one was complaining; no one was dragging their feet. Everyone was there because they were there by choice, to help people." *– Nate Johnson* }

Nate credits Hands On Nashville for providing him with opportunities to contribute to the flood relief.

"I wouldn't have been out there doing anything without knowing what was going on, and that was facilitated through [HON]," he said. He used the organization's website to learn about volunteer site locations throughout the week, and he was impressed with the project-oriented approach that allowed volunteers to choose the type of service they wanted to join.

A native of Maryland, Nate has called Nashville home for only 3 ½ years; but he felt a close connection to the local community through his volunteer efforts, working with the same people at different projects who all remembered his name.

For Nate, the Nashville flood still brings to mind images of destruction; but he said the lasting memories will be of how everyone came together for a common purpose. "It's a pretty rare occurrence that a city organizes its own volunteers in the midst of a disaster, and that will stay in the books for awhile," Nate said.

COME TOGETHER

TO OPERATE A VOLUNTEER RECEPTION CENTER
OUT OF THE ARTHOUSE GARDENS

The only things East Nashvillians Catherine McTamaney and Alan Murdock had in common was their passion for their neighborhood, and both stayed plugged into community happenings through the East Nashville e-mail group. All that changed on May 2, 2010.

Catherine had spent Saturday afternoon with her family at a community theater production in Franklin, followed by a 3 ½-hour drive in the pouring rain to Donelson to perform in a play. Sunday morning after a trip to her basement, she found what most East Nashvillians found – water.

Alan, a landscaper and owner of ArtHouse Gardens, was dealing with a foot injury, and since it was raining, he decided to go home and rest. Alan recalled looking out his window and seeing the water coming down his driveway. "I thought, 'this isn't good.' I realized there were going to be many homes with issues. I put out a message on our listserv asking people to meet at ArtHouse on Monday morning to help clean up. I thought we'd spend the day pumping water out of basements."

One of the first people to respond to Alan's message was Catherine. A professor at Vanderbilt University's Peabody College of Education and Human Development, she had just finished the spring semester, so she had some free time on her hands.

"I e-mailed Alan back and told him I was willing to help. He asked me to answer the phone at ArtHouse Gardens, and direct him and the other East Nashville volunteers to the homes that needed help. As the day went on and the waters rose, the situation became more significant in our community."

"Monday morning, when we showed up at the garden center, it was basically people who had damage to their homes," Alan said. "We started going house to house, and that's when people started saying, 'I have this going on at my house, and would you mind helping me after I help you?' or 'I heard what you guys are doing, and I want to help; but I need some help, too.' We realized that we needed to help each other get the damage taken care of."

ArtHouse Gardens ended up being command central for the East Nashville flood response. Hands On Nashville heard about the community's volunteer efforts and the need for more help. HON asked Alan if ArtHouse would become an official HON Volunteer Reception Center so the organization could send more volunteers to aid East Nashville, and Alan agreed.

Catherine was responsible for organizing all the volunteers and for keeping a database of who needed assistance and what type of help was needed.

- Catherine (far right) directs volunteers at ArtHouse. -

"Catherine was amazing in collecting the information and organizing this incredibly dedicated group of people," Alan said. "We'd stay up until 3 or 4 a.m. e-mailing each other to plan for the next day. She's super-organized. I've never seen anything quite like it."

The first day, around 20 volunteers helped in the neighborhood, and by the end of the week more than 900 volunteers were deployed throughout East Nashville. Over the course of two weeks, approximately 1,700 volunteers came through the ArtHouse Gardens Volunteer Reception Center, and more than 300 homes were served.

"I don't think anyone engaged in the response could walk away from it unchanged," Catherine said. "The volunteers were just incredible people. I think that if there's one thing having shared this experience with my community has left me with, it is a much more profound understanding of how good people are. We saw extraordinary devastation, and what fixed it were neighbors who stood up and said 'I can help.'"

- Dan kayaks through a residential area to help flood survivors. -

PADDLE TO THE
RESCUE

While the vast majority of volunteers after the May floods helped when the water cleared, Dan Gislao used his love for kayaking to help rescue pets and belongings by water.

He woke Monday morning, May 3, thinking he was going to help flood victims clean out their basements, like many other fellow East Nashvillians. But then he used his hobby as an asset. Water was high, and helping on foot was nearly impossible.

When Dan showed up at the ArtHouse Gardens in East Nashville, he brought a couple of bilge pumps, tools that kayakers use to get the water out of their kayaks. He was thinking these would be good for pumping water out of houses. He headed out with a group of volunteers and then got a call from Catherine McTamaney, a volunteer coordinator in East Nashville who worked in concert with Hands On Nashville. "You've got a kayak, right?"

she asked. And this is where his heart and passion for paddling came into play.

When Dan got the call, he was at the home of an avid animal lover in East Nashville who let him borrow a few pet carriers. He strapped a carrier onto the front of his kayak and started his mission. The first area he came to, police officers were ordering people away, so he ventured over to the intersection of Cooper Terrace and Cooper Lane.

Dan heard a scream come from one of the Cooper Terrace residents, "My baby, my baby. My baby is in that house, you've got to go help her!" Dan panicked, logically assuming an infant was inside. But another resident calmly told him it was the woman's little white dog that was in danger. Dan grabbed the pet carrier he had tied to the front of his kayak and brought the dog to safety.

"She was very appreciative. Everyone was. In the Cooper Terrace area, I was helping folks get their animals, medicine, musical instruments, clothes, laptops and whatever else they needed. Some would give me a list, their address and keys." Some just wanted him to go in their house and take pictures and come back and show the damage that had occurred. Unbeknownst to Dan, address-bearing mailboxes were under the water, so it took some time getting to the correct houses.

"People would call or stop by and ask if we could check on relatives and elderly neighbors. You didn't really think about what you were doing until you were done doing it. Once you were home, showered, and had dinner you thought about what you saw that day. It didn't hit you until you sat down. It was all so surreal."

There are many interesting situations that Dan encountered. One woman came up to him and said that her father had passed away and the only pictures she had of him were in a photo album in her house. She asked him to go get it for her. "These were family heirlooms. You can rebuild a house, but you can't get back some of these things."

"I was helping folks get their animals, medicine, musical instruments, clothes, laptops and whatever else they needed. Some would give me a list, their address and keys."

–Dan Gislao

- The General Jackson Showboat floats parallel with Dan in an East Nashville neighborhood. -

In another instance, as Dan was paddling house to house gathering belongings, he turned his head and there sat the General Jackson Showboat. "Right there. Right over my shoulder. The river was so high that you couldn't distinguish where the river began or ended."

"On one hand, it was very upsetting seeing what was going on all around me. On the other, it was a good feeling of satisfaction knowing you are helping people and making a difference. Emotions were just pulling me in every direction," Dan said. "Morale was great – no conflicts, no egos. Just true volunteerism."

Dan encountered many uplifting moments during the days of the flood cleanup and rescue; but when asked, he talked about the weeks and months after the flood. He and his girlfriend went to walk their dog in June, a month after the flood, around areas that Dan had helped. One of the families for whom he snapped pictures was moving back into their house. Dan went up to talk with the family members. They remembered him, and it brought great joy.

"It felt so good seeing people positive and moving back in—they had no self-pity. Not one bit."

- Dan shows a flood survivor images of her water soaked home. -

PASTOR & HIS CHURCH PUT

COMMITMENT TO OTHERS

~ AHEAD OF THEMSELVES ~

When the Rev. Harold Moses Love Jr. heard that members of his St. Paul A.M.E. Church congregation wanted to commit a day to making meals for those affected by the flood in the Bordeaux community, he had no idea that their church would become one of the area's designated centers for flood relief.

- Rev. Harold Love meets with Sen. Harper and another community leader in St. Paul A.M.E. Church. -

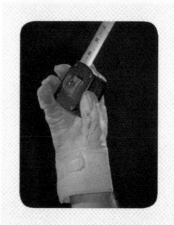

The church wanted to set up in a central location, but learned that many areas were inaccessible due to the flood's rising waters. Members decided to cook in the church parking lot, but realized, as the day progressed, that many people were not able to reach them.

"Early in the day, we weren't aware of the extent of the damage," Harold said. "I suggested that we go deliver food, and we just got in the back of a pickup truck passing out food and water."

As he saw the devastation of the flood, Harold, who has a special love for Bordeaux, was deeply troubled. He had grown up in the area and his father, Harold Love Sr., (who served on the Metro Council from 1962-68 and as a state representative from 1968-94) would often take him along to talk with constituents and participate in community service projects. As an adult, Harold Jr. became active as a volunteer, serving on several boards in the Nashville community and as pastor of St. Paul for nine years.

Harold knew it would take more than cooking food to help his community. His church had 50 members, and of them, 25 were adults and many were aging. How could they make a larger impact?

"We just needed to have a will and the Lord would make everything come together. People would show up," Harold said. "When you drive down West Hamilton Avenue and see that cabinets and beds are out in front yards, and trees and cars are turned over, you have to ask yourself, 'How are these people going to make it unless I come help?' So, I asked our volunteers if they could come back for one more day."

The next day, the church was surprised to receive bottled water, supplies and monetary donations.

> "Seeing the floodwaters and the houses in the area really shook me. I thought, 'That could have been my family.' These were my friends, my teachers, my classmates, their parents and their grandparents. Some friends who lived out of town were calling me to say, 'Thank you for looking out for my grandmother.'"
> – Rev. Harold Love

"I didn't know how we would continue to get supplies," Harold said, "but I told everyone, 'Let's just keep showing up every day and see what happens.' So, we kept showing up, and we stayed late."

Everyone at St. Paul made sacrifices to keep the doors open for those in need. Edna Earle Burney, the church musician, lost her vehicles and had considerable flood damage to her home, but still came to help in the relief effort. Harold, who is studying to obtain a Ph.D. in public administration at Tennessee State University, was in the middle of finals week and decided to receive an incomplete in his classes in order to be able to help at the church.

"Mrs. Burney was here on Sunday morning, in position to play the piano. She inspired us and reminded us that people have the faith to trust that it's going to be alright, and that they have to look for a better day," Harold said. "I could get an incomplete in my class, but I couldn't get an incomplete in helping someone."

The small church became a larger resource center through discussions with Metro Council members, Hands On Nashville, the Nashville Branch of the NAACP, the Nashville Red Cross, the Department of Homeland Security, the Nashville Chapter of the National Association of Black Journalists, Waste Management, FEMA and A.M.E. church leaders. By the weekend, the church had received enough clothes and cleanup kits to fill rooms in the church from floor to ceiling, and food donations continued to come in from local restaurants and community service organizations. Volunteers from Hands On Nashville, churches and community agencies came to help distribute supplies and prepare food.

"Volunteers were excited and eager to help. Other churches on our street were inaccessible or damaged from the flood. By divine mandate, we were – our church that sits on a hill – left to do the work, and we decided to do it," Harold said. "I don't think any of the volunteers would have exchanged the opportunity to go to bed at night knowing they helped somebody, and made a difference, for anything in the world."

AN OUTLET FOR
GIVING

For Bonnie Duckworth, the secretary at Bellevue Church of Christ during the time of the May 2010 flood in Nashville, the response to the aftermath renewed her faith in mankind. It was a time when she encountered total strangers, not only from Nashville, but also from as far away as California and New York who without being asked would call and say, "I want to help, here's what I'm doing, and I'm coming."

- Bonnie leads volunteers to their River Plantation work sites. -

Bonnie embodied this selfless spirit in her daily commitment to making the church a hub for relief efforts in support of River Plantation and Beech Bend, two of the hardest-hit communities. In the days and weeks after the flood, Bellevue Church of Christ offered up its Fellowship Hall, and eventually its gym, to house a grocery store and space for furniture and cleaning supplies to donate to flood victims.

The church's parking lot was used to shuttle volunteers, including those organized by Hands On Nashville, to work sites every 15 minutes, for which Bonnie and church staff relied on the generosity of other local churches to supply buses and drivers. The church also partnered with Service International, a Missouri-based nonprofit organization that specializes in disaster relief, to provide volunteers with the tools and leadership necessary to clean and restore homes at the work sites. In total, somewhere between 2,000 and 3,000 volunteers were organized thanks to these collaborations.

"I have volunteered for many years, from the American Cancer Society to the Special Olympics to TPAC [Tennessee Performing Arts Center], and organized large events; but never had I worked with anything like the flood," Bonnie said. "In fact, I don't know any of us who would ever have had the experience of doing that, unless you were in the rescue-recovery mode, so you just stepped up and did what you had to do."

"I don't know if I could have coped like I saw other people cope. It was unbelievable to see the courage they had. I think if anything will make you say, 'I will be a better person, because I've seen people step up and do what they've done' – I saw it. I get teary-eyed thinking about them." – *Bonnie Duckworth*

Reflective of her giving nature, Bonnie ignored much of her own recovery needs in order to continue organizing this community-relief effort, and was touched when others took it upon themselves to do things for her, such as replant her home garden before it was too late in the season.

In fact, her tireless efforts, including 17-hour days, seven days a week, prompted friends to urge her to take days off. However, Bonnie is self-described as "high-energy," and no matter what, she was back at the church, leading the effort. "You know, they nicknamed me 'The General,' 'General Duckworth.' ... [They'd say,] 'The General's going to coordinate this,'" Bonnie said, laughing. "The funny thing is, when we started hearing about the flood in Brisbane, Australia, where our church is now contributing to the relief effort, we'd hear stories about their own General Duckworth. I couldn't believe it!"

Looking back over this extraordinary span of her life, Bonnie cites being continually amazed – by the volunteers' generosity and by the courage and strength of those who lost so much.

DAY OF VOLUNTEERING BECOMES

A WAY OF LIFE

~~~~~~~~~~

When the floods hit, LaQuita Summey knew she couldn't just sit at home and watch the news on television. She had to get out and do something.

She made her way to the East Nashville Volunteer Reception Center and was impressed with what she saw – not only were volunteers providing food and water to flood victims, they had already moved beyond those basic functions and were collecting clothes, organizing home assessments and cataloging residents' needs. LaQuita was just a face in the crowd that first afternoon – helping with whatever the organizers needed.

It was a long day, she was growing tired, ready to go back home. Then she received a call from a friend in North Nashville. "LaQuita, you've got to get over here," her friend said. "It's sheer chaos." Then another call; the occupants of a rental property in North Nashville that LaQuita owned and managed with her husband were on the line, and they were in a panic – the water was rising fast.

So the stay-at-home mom and graduate student with four courses remaining before she earned her degree in public administration decided not to go home that afternoon; instead, she drove over to North Nashville and volunteered some more. To anyone who would listen, her message was the same: Tell me what to do, and I'll do it. Today, I'm all yours.

Since then, her son has blessed her with her first grandchild, her graduate studies have been put on hold, and what began as a day of volunteering has turned into a life's mission.

Long after the flood waters had receded, after the dignitaries had returned to Washington, D.C., after the media had turned to new stories and even after many Nashvillians had returned to their "normal" lives, LaQuita Summey was volunteering more than 100 hours per week to help finish the work that she and thousands of volunteers started on that day in May 2010.

– LaQuita (center) with her North Nashville Flood Relief Team. –

After arriving at the North Nashville corner of West Hamilton and Tucker Road, LaQuita was prepared to be just one of many volunteers, as she had in East Nashville. But it soon became apparent that a leader was needed, and LaQuita was approached: Would she coordinate Hands On Nashville's Volunteer Reception Center there?

"I prayed about it, spoke to my husband about it, and he said, 'If you really want to do this, do it.' So she said 'yes,' and soon was organizing an effort that would come to include more than 4,100 volunteers, most of whom were pointed to the North Nashville Flood Relief site by Hands On Nashville.

These volunteers were largely assigned to assess more than 200 flood-damaged homes and take on the laborious process of gutting them out: knocking down and ripping out drywall, pulling out damaged insulation, removing furniture, clearing out debris, mitigating mold, scrubbing floors and windows, and salvaging personal belongings.

"The reward is when you see the smiles on the faces of the people you've helped. They're really grateful that someone is still there when they don't know where to turn. They have confidence in the work that we do, and that means everything."
— LaQuita Summey

As days turned to weeks and then to months, LaQuita was impressed with the outpouring of support from volunteers, not only those from Nashville, but folks from as far away as Michigan and Pennsylvania who are still driving down to Nashville to help out, and college students spending their spring breaks working on drywall in North Nashville rather than their tans in sunny Florida.

The 100-hour weeks were challenging for LaQuita and her family; she won't deny that. Rather than spending time with her daughter at home, she often found them bonding at The Home Depot when they were out purchasing carpeting or linoleum for a damaged home. But the rewards were richer than she ever imagined.

"At times, it can be challenging as a wife and a mother and a grandmother – there are definitely moments when it seems overwhelming," she said. "But so many people lost so much, and some people lost everything. One woman told me, 'I had 45 years of memories that I lost in 45 seconds.' It's so hard for people to recover from something like that. So the reward is when you see the smiles on the faces of the people you've helped. They're really grateful that someone is still there when they don't know where to turn. They have confidence in the work that we do, and that means everything."

All hands on deck:

FAMILIES

REALIZE THE POWER OF SERVICE

The first week of May 2010, more than 123,000 prospective volunteers visited Hands On Nashville's website to view hundreds of flood-related service projects. Many were families who later found themselves volunteering. The Trail and Ward families were among their ranks.

The Trail Family

Stephanie Trail wanted to pitch in and help alongside her husband and their two young children. She recalled, "I was looking for projects in parts of town that had the least number of volunteers – where we were most needed. I also wanted to give my kids an opportunity to give back. As a parent, I think it's really important to teach how important it is to take care of each other. If someone needs help, you should help them out."

On May 5, Stephanie and Robert, along with 8-year-old Jazlyn and 5-year-old R.J., entered the parking lot of Pearl Cohn High School. Stephanie's brother and his girlfriend joined them. They stayed for five hours, distributing cases of water to every flood victim who drove through the lot.

R.J. said, "I helped open the car doors to get the water in the cars." Jazlyn followed with, "I sat on my uncle's shoulders, and he told cars which way to go." It's clear this experience made an impression.

"I liked helping people who needed it," said Jazlyn. "If there was another flood like this, I would do the same; go help people. I felt glad about what I did."

The Ward Family

May 8, 2010, was Mother's Day – a day that Rich Ward and his younger sons, then ages 6 and 12, will never forget. Together, they went to North Nashville's volunteer hub to complete the project for which Rich signed up via Hands On Nashville's website.

Rich said he "brought his sons thinking it would be a good experience for them to spend an afternoon helping out some less fortunate people. Had I realized what we were getting into, I probably would have left them home."

The devastation he saw on and around West Hamilton Avenue was more than he expected. He was worried about his sons' capacity to deal with the wreckage.

Those fears were quickly washed away by the positive energy of other volunteers who represented every walk of life. "I've never been so proud of those two boys. They dug in like everyone else."

Rich and his sons were moved.

"The full impact of the experience didn't hit me until hours after we had left," Rich said. "We had taken my mother out to dinner for Mother's Day, and we were on our way home. The memory passed through my mind of a family standing in their driveway, next to their mud-covered car, applauding us as we drove away."

"We did help. We did make a difference."

- RJ. and Jazlyn Trail create directional signs at a water distribution center. -

MARKET RECOVERY

As the floodwaters crept up Rosa Parks Boulevard toward the Nashville Farmers' Market, Jeff Themm had two main concerns, which were somewhat at odds with each other.

One was the evacuation of the building's tenants, not only for their immediate safety, but also so they could get home to help protect their families.

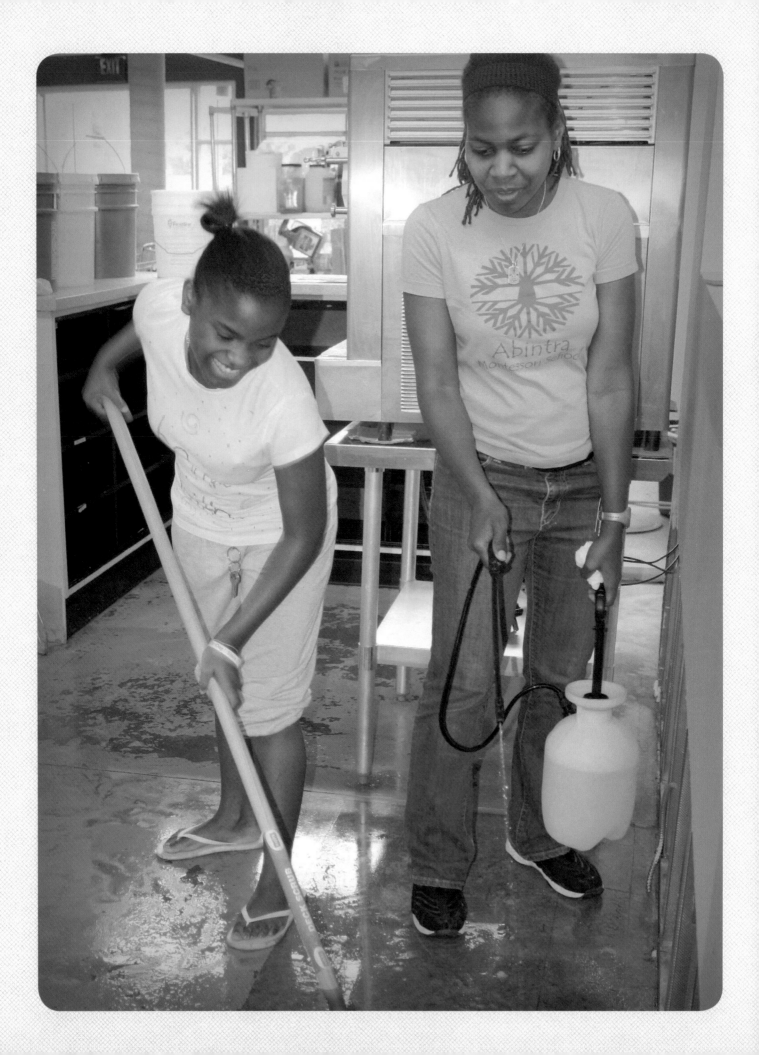

The second concern was the unattended produce, merchandise and equipment that had to be left behind. As 18 inches of floodwater filled the Farmers' Market on that Sunday in early May, its director had no idea what the immediate future would hold.

What he did know was that he was going to need a lot of help. And that help arrived the next morning in the form of Hands On Nashville volunteers, who showed up ready to provide their services in any way necessary.

"I didn't know much about Hands On Nashville until we needed them, but they became vital for all of us as they served a great need to help restore the Farmers' Market as well as the whole city," Jeff said.

At the Farmers' Market, the volunteers worked tirelessly in order to accomplish a great number of tasks quickly and efficiently, from general cleanup to fixing electrical outlets to removing and replacing drywall. Without them, Jeff said, the market would never have been able to recover as quickly as it did.

"There was nothing too dirty or too hard for them to do," he said. "They put a mask on, put gloves on and went to work."

With the efforts of Jeff, the Farmers' Market staff and the volunteers, the market was able to recover and reopen only a week after the flood. In the process, Jeff learned all he needed to know about Hands On Nashville.

"Hands On Nashville is primed to be an organization that can be there for Nashville," he said, "for whatever we may need in the future."

MEMORIES of, SHARING & LOVE

A volunteer ran over to Scott Mattingly, a 24-year-old volunteer turned Hands On Nashville site manager in charge of leading a flood relief team. "What do you want to do with the water bottles?" he asked Scott. No one had told Scott that water was being delivered, but he assumed someone in a pick-up truck was just making a friendly donation.

As he followed the volunteer around the corner, Scott stopped in his tracks. There were two semi-trucks loaded down with 24-packs of water bottles. Scott was amazed and shocked, but things like that kept happening to him.

"Nothing happened because of me," Scott said. "It was no skill or talent. When I needed something, there it was in front of me. When I needed a water truck, it would just appear."

That was the case in many instances. Community members would see volunteers' needs and fill them without needing to be asked. Everyone offered the resources they could to keep powering the masses of humanity who volunteered to help those impacted by the flood to recover.

Scott started volunteering as soon as the waters began to rise. He was without power, but his house stayed dry, so he took in his neighbors' pets. His next door neighbors fed him oatmeal when food was running low. Just as Nashville joined forces as a city, Scott's neighbors embraced each other, helping any way that they could.

As soon as the water receded, Scott headed out to River Plantation because he knew the area needed volunteers. In the first few days, Scott learned how to demolish a wall and rip up carpet.

A few days later, Scott found himself teaching others the same skills. For the next few weeks, Scott agreed to be a full-time volunteer manager. He was now teaching other volunteers how to safely

- Scott speaks with a community volunteer about the day's work. -

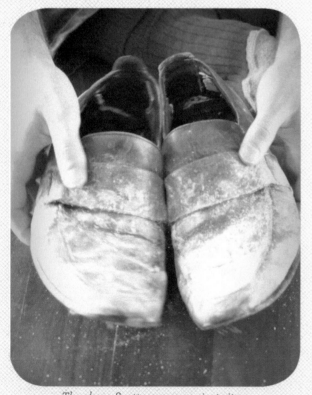

- The shoes Scott wore on project sites. -

demolish walls, which prevented the flooded homes from molding. Scott said he was the most exhausted he had ever been in his life. "It was a joyful exhaustion," said Scott. "The more tired I was, the happier I was that day."

One thing that Scott really tried to emphasize to volunteer teams was safety. "People were dealing with wastewater and cutting carpets out. I wanted to make sure they were aware of their surroundings and acted with caution."

Morale during the flood relief was surprisingly high. He loved seeing entire businesses take the day off to come help out. Parents would often bring their entire families. "Of course an 8-year-old can't demolish a wall," Scott said, "but they can help hand out food and water. It was great seeing citizenship in action."

"IT WAS A CHANCE TO SEE LOVE POURED OUT BY PEOPLE OF EVERY RACE, SEX, AGE AND RELIGION, EVERY GROUP YOU COULD IMAGINE."

– Scott Mattingly

Scott describes that time of his life as vibrant. Long after the flood, Scott was discovering crumpled receipts or scraps of paper with notes about which houses to assist. He received letter after letter thanking him for his time, love and help in a moment of need.

"I love that I still find those things because it reminds me of that point in my life. It was larger than life. Not in the negative way we see from images of people's homes; but it was a chance to see love poured out by people of every race, sex, age and religion, every group you could imagine."

"This isn't something that beat us down that we need to put behind us," said Scott. "It's something that brought about a change in our community, and that is something worth commemorating."

TIME & LEADERSHIP

WHAT ONE MTSU STUDENT LEARNED ABOUT HIMSELF WHILE STUDYING FOR EXAMS

Every college student knows what the month of May is like – cramming for exams and racing to complete the many papers and final projects required by professors. That was definitely the case for Jared McGowan, a 22-year-old student and Army ROTC participant at Middle Tennessee State University. The difference was Jared didn't let those things stand in his way when Mayor Karl Dean called for volunteers to combat Nashville's flooding.

On May 3, Jared joined hundreds of volunteers to sandbag Nashville's MetroCenter levies. "We set up five human chains about 50 to 60 yards long, passing sandbags for hours, well into the night," he said. "We unloaded eight to 10 Dumpsters-full of sandbags and made a wall about four feet high at two locations."

Spending hours sandbagging might sound like a chore, but not for Jared. It was a start of his spree of flood-response volunteerism. During the next few weeks, he mucked out houses on West Hamilton Avenue in North Nashville and throughout Bellevue – from River Plantation to its surrounding neighborhoods. He led volunteers on door-to-door wellness checks in Antioch, ensuring homes were evacuated and that flood-relief information was distributed.

And, he did much more.

"The most uplifting thing I saw was a picnic at a Bellevue Park organized by area residents for their neighbors and volunteers. These people's homes had been practically demolished, but they threw this huge picnic. There was a band, all kinds of food, kids playing, and neighbors congregating and having a good time. Although many had lost everything tangible, their optimism remained intact. Their gratitude for volunteers was enormous."

Throughout this time, Jared was taking exams and commuting back and forth from MTSU. He also was holding down a job. It was this level of beyond-the-call-of-duty commitment that made Jared a focus of a "Making a Difference" feature about Hands On Nashville on NBC Nightly News. In hearing his story, it was clear that Jared did not participate in these volunteer efforts for recognition. He is just the type of selfless person who enjoys helping people in need.

> "I've always liked to volunteer, and this close to home, you just have to. Nashville is my city, and I needed to help fix it. That's how my mom raised me, and that's what the Army taught me." – *Jared McGowan*

- Jared McGowan volunteers in River Plantation. -

TENNESSEE TITANS DEFINED

TEAMWORK

A hard-charging Tennessee Titan can deliver quite a wallop on the football field. So imagine what would happen if you gave 45 of them sledgehammers, crowbars and other wrecking equipment and turned them loose to do demolition.

- Kerry Collins deconstructs a West Nashville home. -

That's what happened in May 2010 when the players and another 35 Titans administrators and coaches arrived by the busload in West Nashville to help clean up flood-damaged homes. The effort was arranged through Hands On Nashville.

"When I was a kid, I used to imagine what it would be like to tear down a house – just to tear something up," recalled linebacker Gerald McRath, one of the players who helped with the flood cleanup effort. "This gave me a chance to see what it was like."

The task assigned to the team members was to tear out walls, appliances, trim and other damaged parts of homes to prevent them becoming mold-infested.

The work done by McRath and his teammates was not the dream demolition he envisioned in his childhood, however. He said the horrible smell of mildewing houses, the sadness of the homes' residents and the amount of work that needed to be done were almost overwhelming.

"By the end of the day, you are kind of sad, but at least feel good to have helped someone," McRath recalled.

Like teammate and quarterback Kerry Collins, McRath had pitched in during a major crisis before. He said he was on the University of Southern Mississippi team when Hurricane Katrina hit that area. He and teammates rolled up their sleeves to help. Collins was the New York Giants quarterback when the 9/11 attacks occurred in Manhattan, and he lent his time to comforting survivors in the aftermath of that event.

Punter Brett Kern, on the other hand, said he had never witnessed such a serious tragedy before he volunteered for the cleanup effort.

"The people in the neighborhood were waving and smiling and yelling, 'Thank you,'" Kern said. "Your heart really goes out to them. I don't know if I could handle something like that as well as they did. It made me feel very blessed."

Titans long snapper Ken Amato said he was impressed by the large number of Nashvillians who showed up in flood-ravaged areas, trying to help others.

"This is the Volunteer State, and you could tell it on those days. Large groups of people were walking through the area, asking if anyone needed help," said Amato, who had helped clean after Hurricane Andrew when he lived in Florida and accompanied teammate Nick Harper to do more flood cleanup work after tackling the West Nashville project.

> "I have done volunteer work before, but nothing on this grand a scale. Just about everyone from the team was involved, and that made it very special, very unique."
> – Titans Quarterback Kerry Collins

Collins recalled that Titans Senior Executive Vice President Steve Underwood and former head coach Jeff Fisher were instrumental in pulling together the volunteer effort, encouraging others to take part.

Collins was so revved up by the West Nashville cleanup experience that he volunteered to join a church-organized residential cleanup effort in the Bellevue area a few days later.

"The rest of the world could learn from what happened in Nashville on those days," Collins said. "The whole city pulled together to help those who lost everything."

McRath said, "This says a lot about the Titans organization that they did something like that. There is a bond you get with the community you play for, and we wanted to help. This tragedy could have happened to anyone. It just hits home with you when you see it."

- *Becky Seip behind the lens.* -

FOCUSING ON RELIEF

In high school, Becky Seip received her first 35-millimeter camera as a gift from her parents. Several decades and cameras later, she has given her own gift of topnotch free photography as she volunteers hours and hours of her time to Nashville's nonprofits.

Becky is one of the reasons the tremendous volunteer effort during the flood of 2010 is a well-documented phenomenon in the form of thousands of dramatic pictures.

A former professional photographer, Becky received her college degree in photography and worked as a photographer for years, including a stint at the Wildhorse Saloon. When she became disabled a few years ago, she began donating her time and skills to numerous nonprofits in the area, including Hands On Nashville, the Nashville Humane Association and the Nashville Zoo.

"I love to help the agencies," Becky said. "Despite my disability, I wanted to continue my photography work, and I found volunteering was the perfect way to do that."

Becky began volunteering for HON in 2009, when she took photos of activities surrounding Hands On Nashville Day, which is the city's largest day of service in Metro Nashville Public Schools. Since then, she's taken photos of events ranging from the Martin Luther King Jr. Day of Service to youth book-sorting projects.

Immediately following the May 2010 flood, Becky volunteered her skills as a photographer nearly every day for several weeks. As the cleanup turned into a rebuilding effort, she continued to volunteer approximately once a week and today still gives her time and talent to HON when needed.

"I couldn't do the physical labor required at so many of the cleanup sites, but I could volunteer my photography skills," said Becky. "I knew the volunteer response after the flood needed documentation, so I called up Hands On Nashville to see how I could help."

Becky visited nearly every part of Nashville affected by the flood to take photos. She first realized the overwhelming devastation of the flood when she drove to Moss Rose Drive in East Nashville, a mere half-mile from her own home, to take photos of the rising water.

"It was shocking to see," Becky said. "The street runs parallel to the Cumberland River, and water was just pouring into people's homes. You couldn't tell where the river stopped and people's yards began. Hearing the homeowners talk about having to be rescued from the second and third stories of their homes was unbelievable."

She vividly recalled the day she spent with several members of the Tennessee Titans as they volunteered their time to clean up in West Nashville. "They all worked so hard and really had fun under the circumstances. They showed great teamwork and did anything that needed to be done."

Becky's photos have been released by HON to more than 20 local, regional and national media outlets and have appeared everywhere from the CMT Music Awards to a Community Foundation of Middle Tennessee newsletter. In fact, many of the photos in this book are hers.

LAUNDRY FOR 40,000?
CAN DO IT

T he Nike Factory Store in Opry Mills mall was one of 2,773 Nashville businesses that sustained flood damage in May 2010. And like many Nashville individuals and businesses hit by losses, the store's owners and employees responded with giving instead of placing themselves first. Store manager Beth Sesler recalls how volunteers just started contributing to what turned out to be one of Nashville's biggest clothing giveaways.

"It was several days before we could even get access to the store. We had to wait for water to recede," she said. "We went in, and the first thing I remember is the emotion of knowing how much labor went into putting the store together. And, now, it seemed like it was all in vain."

Beth said there had been two feet of water in the store, that merchandise above that level had absorbed water, "and even the paper in the shirts was wet."

"The easiest thing we could have done, and the quickest thing as far as remediation for the space was concerned, would have been to destroy all of the merchandise," she added.

Doing what's easy is not always what's right. Beth saw an opportunity. Their destiny became the organization of a communitywide volunteer project that placed the store's 40,000 pieces of merchandise in the hands of flood-impacted families served by Metro Nashville Public Schools and local charities. The process of preparing the Nike Factory Store's clothing for donation had begun.

Beth's team took merchandise from their store. Under a circus tent set up in the Opry Mills parking lot, they removed clothing tags, sorted the items by size, bagged the merchandise and placed it in eight portable storage units.

Then, the soiled product needed to be laundered. Beth sought cost estimates, and she connected with UniFirst, a uniform and work wear provider. To her delight, they stepped up to handle this enormous laundry project.

UniFirst general manager Chris Neeley said, "We were particularly eager to contribute to the volunteer efforts launched to help those who suddenly found themselves with nothing."

With the storage units full of clean clothing, the massive re-sorting and arranging effort began. Beth recalls, "When you're dealing with 40,000 units, that's a huge chore. That's T-shirts, pants and jackets. We also had socks, which probably was the biggest challenge for my team. When you talk about mating 8,000 units of socks, you can imagine. I mean, you do it at home, and there's always that missing sock. I think out of 8,000 units, we had three missing socks. So we did pretty well on that."

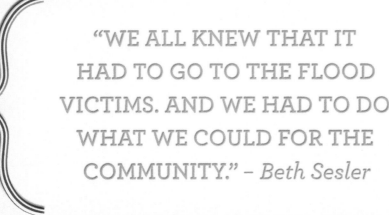

{ "WE ALL KNEW THAT IT HAD TO GO TO THE FLOOD VICTIMS. AND WE HAD TO DO WHAT WE COULD FOR THE COMMUNITY." – *Beth Sesler* }

Working in concert with Hands On Nashville, Metro Nashville Public Schools and the Federal Emergency Management Agency, a giant clothing giveaway event was planned for McGavock Elementary School. Metro Schools students, faculty and their families, along with other flood-impacted households served by Catholic Charities of Tennessee, St. Paul A.M.E. Church and Bellevue Church of Christ, were invited to attend.

On May 28, about 2,000 people entered McGavock Elementary School's gym to take advantage of this generous offer, receiving 10 articles of clothing and six pairs of socks per member of each household.

A 150-member volunteer team was there to support Nike's vision and ensure a special shopping experience – free of charge – that was equivalent to shopping at a Nike store.

"We served as personal shoppers, and each flood victim or family that came in that day had a personal shopper help find their products," Beth said. "We were able to match items for them to put an outfit together, and I think that's what made the event very special."

Beth, who has done other volunteer work ever since she was a child, said the delighted reaction from children that day is something she will remember the rest of her life.

– A Smithson Craighead Academy student watches as volunteers landscape his school. –

VOLUNTEERS BRING ELEMENTARY SCHOOL
BACK TO LIFE

Twelve classrooms. The gym. The cafeteria. All of it – flooded.

Spaces that just days before had enjoyed the wonderful rambunctiousness of elementary school kids were now covered in mud and muck and other remnants from Nashville's historic flood of 2010.

That's the vision that appears in Sister Mary Acerbi's mind when she replays the post-flood moments of May 2010.

Like so many other places in Middle Tennessee, this was the scene at Smithson Craighead Academy, Nashville's first charter school, which serves 250 at-risk children who had previously been struggling in the classroom.

The school, housed in an old building in need of occasional repair and beautification projects, had a relationship with Hands On Nashville prior to the flood. Just days after the rains came, seemingly attempting to drown her city, Sister Mary, who serves as property manager (among other things) at the school, knew just whom to call to help bring her school back to life.

"We don't have the money to do the types of repairs that were needed after the flood," recalls Sister Mary. "Hands On Nashville sent hundreds of volunteers to our school to help us. I was awed by it."

Among those who came to help was Kathleen Pearson, who led a group from Waller Lansden Dortch & Davis, LLP. A team of 25, from summer associates to partners in the firm, spent the better part of a day at the school pulling up dirty, molded carpet.

"It was very hard work," Kathleen said. "But we had a willing and eager team and morale was very high that day. We had smaller teams in each room and everyone was challenging one another to get the really stuck pieces of carpet up. It was quite a team-building experience for us. We were literally cheering for one another as one person would whack with the shovel, then several others would pull with all their might."

At the end of the day, while they were exhausted, they also felt uplifted. "We felt, well, dirty, but we also felt awesome," Kathleen said, with a huge smile on her face. "It was a really great day. We all knew we had helped a group of people who really needed it."

The work at Smithson Craighead continued.

More volunteers entered the school, including a group from Creative Artists Agency, an international talent agency better known as CAA.

Said CAA's Brett Saliba, "CAA brought our Nashville, New York and Los Angeles offices together to help the school's recovery process. We painted and landscaped, building upon the volunteer work that had already been completed."

The CAA team, with leadership from art expert and fellow volunteer Linda Anderson, used their creative skills to add large-scale murals to the exteriors of portable classrooms. They also completed other indoor and outdoor painting projects and landscaped the school's courtyard, adding plants and a picnic area.

"Without volunteers, we would not be able to continue our program," said Sister Mary. "Watching so much work happen in such a short amount of time was really beautiful. It brought tears to my eyes. We could never have done it without Hands On Nashville. Never."

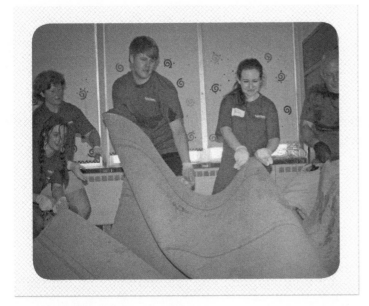

"Hands On Nashville sent hundreds of volunteers to our school to help us. I was awed by it." — *Sister Mary Acerbi*

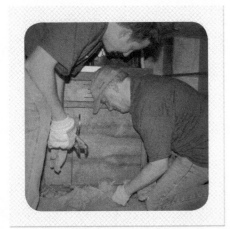

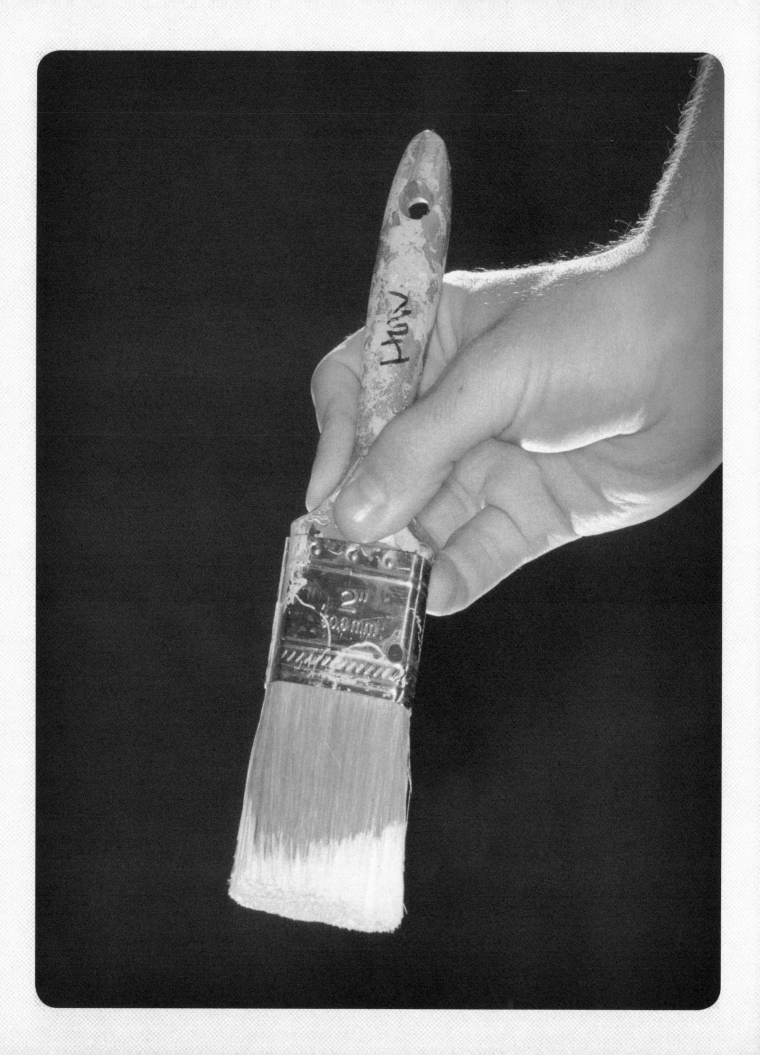

NON-STOP HERO

Jesse McIntyre not only knows how to drive home a nail. He also knows how to drive home the meaning of great community volunteerism. An experienced construction worker, Jesse logged more than 800 hours of service in the weeks following the May flood.

As most Nashvillians were just beginning to realize the widespread destruction of the flood, Jesse was already on his way to Hands On Nashville. Jaclyn Khoury, HON rebuild project manager, remembered the first time Jesse came into her office a few hours after the initial flooding. "He was dressed in work clothes and said, 'I'm ready. How can I help?'"

- *Jesse cleans up debris in a flood survivor's home.* -

Jesse initially assessed homes in hard-hit neighborhoods that required substantial "muck-outs," a term that refers to pulling out all water-logged debris from a person's home, and he personally gutted dozens of homes. He assessed homeowner needs and helped HON identify streets where large volunteer deployments were needed. Jesse also had been trained in grief counseling through a volunteer ministers' program and put that training to work with the many homeowners he encountered directly following the flood.

{ "Even six months after, there were dedicated volunteers who came out to help on the rebuilds. I formed friendships with some of those volunteers, and still see them to this day." – *Jesse McIntyre* }

As Hands On Nashville transitioned its work from recovery to rebuilding, Jesse became a certified Rebuilding Project Leader. In this role, he led 700-plus volunteers in the restoration of more than 30 homes owned by low-income families.

Jesse was often one of the first to be on the rebuild site, setting up the registration tent before the rest of the volunteers arrived, and one of the last to leave, making sure the site was ready for the next day. Through this process, Jesse responsibly managed more than $300,000 in building supplies that were required to restore these homes.

In recognition of his tirelesss work and commitment to the Nashville Community during the flood, Jesse was named one of three finalists for the 2010 Titans Community Quarterback Award.

VETERAN JOURNALISTS
MOVED BY NASHVILLE FLOOD
EXPERIENCE

NBC correspondent Ron Mott and his camera crew provided some of the earliest national media coverage from Nashville of the May 2010 flood, but what started out as a breaking news story turned into a human interest story that was both tragic and uplifting.

As Ron was reporting from Nashville, his producer Terry Pickard was back in the Atlanta regional bureau putting together stories, working with local NBC affiliate WSMV-Channel 4 to get additional footage and doing research on the situation. It was clear to both of them that something special was going on. "We got on the phone to New York and told them we needed to get back to Nashville," Terry said.

"When we came back shortly after doing the initial reporting to do the 'Making A Difference' story for NBC Nightly News," Ron said, "the amount of progress that had been made by volunteers was just unbelievable."

As part of his research, Terry quickly realized that Hands On Nashville was the go-to agency in terms of helping the NBC crew capture the emerging volunteer effort. The crew was led to the devastated Southeast Nashville area, where they were introduced to Jay Vorhees, who was coordinating cleanup assignments from the Antioch United Methodist Church and was among those featured in the "Making A Difference" segment.

"We were witnessing the best of America," Terry said, adding that he was struck by how the tragedy brought together people who normally would not have had contact with each other, especially in the areas around Antioch with large immigrant populations.

"People were giving up their own time to drag muddy, gooey carpets to Dumpsters. There were middle-aged women out there doing heavy lifting. There were people showing up from all over the Southeast, people using their vacation time who said they came to Nashville after seeing our earlier reports.

"There was the college kid (Jared McGowan) who was driving 70 miles a day to volunteer. There were two busloads of Nashville private school kids who gave up their field day of fun and games and came looking for people to help."

For Ron, a seasoned reporter who has covered many disasters, it was impossible to remain an objective observer. "You can't help but get emotionally involved when you are standing there talking to someone with three or four kids and they say they don't know where their next meal is coming from, where they are going to sleep, what they are going to do."

Both Terry and Ron said the Nashville experience was truly special and "unique" – a word that journalists do not throw around lightly.

"What struck us about Hands On Nashville was how fast they were putting people to work where they were needed," Ron said. "I've covered countless disasters where it took days to get people where they were needed, where people would come in from out of town and no one could tell them where to go. Hands On Nashville had it down to a science – it was like watching a machine work, not only in attracting volunteers, but in organizing them and making use of them. You had old people, young people, black, white, rich, poor. It gives me chills just thinking about it."

Terry, a veteran producer, who grew up in Georgia and worked in several TV markets in the South, said the experience reminded him that Southerners as a whole check on their family, friends and colleagues during times of trouble – "they worry about people" – and he believes that this spirit helped drive the outpouring of volunteerism.

Nevertheless, he said, "The response to this was truly amazing. Hands On Nashville deserves a lot of recognition, and so do all the volunteers."

Ron, for his part, hopes Nashville's efforts become a pattern, "a model of how to respond to a natural disaster, because it was a unique response."

"No one had to bark at people to get them going."

> "IT REALLY WARMED MY HEART TO GIVE THESE PEOPLE RECOGNITION – THEY DESERVED THEIR SO-CALLED 15 MINUTES OF FAME."
> – TERRY PICKARD

– NBC's Ron Mott interviews Jared McGowan and Terry Pickard. –

- Capital Records Nashville recording artist Dierks Bentley performs at a

Hands On Nashville and Today Show flood donation event in Bellevue. -

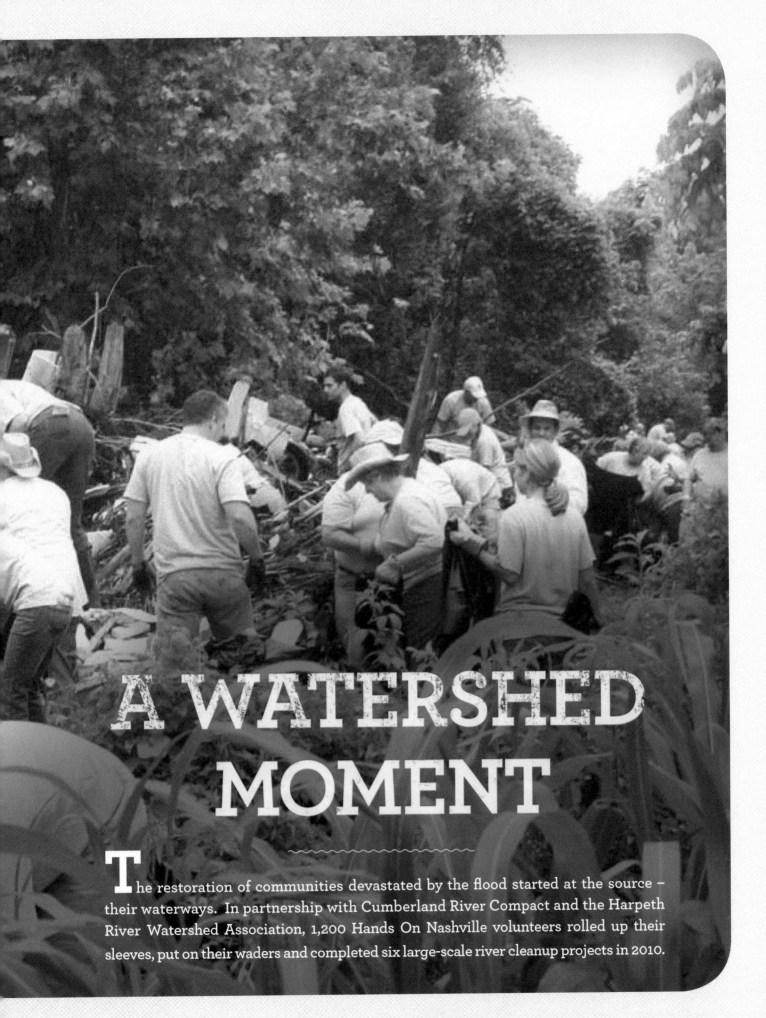

A WATERSHED MOMENT

The restoration of communities devastated by the flood started at the source – their waterways. In partnership with Cumberland River Compact and the Harpeth River Watershed Association, 1,200 Hands On Nashville volunteers rolled up their sleeves, put on their waders and completed six large-scale river cleanup projects in 2010.

Cumberland River Compact & Mill Creek

One of Hands On Nashville's first debris removal projects took place in Mill Creek, located in Southeast Nashville. HON's Amy Maloney met with Doug Hausken of the Cumberland River Compact to determine an access point, develop a cleanup plan and go on a site visit of the creek.

Amy recalled, "We had a team of 400 corporate volunteers from Healthways coming out June 17, and we wanted to be sure we had a project that could occupy several hours of their time and offer a great teamwork experience.

"When I went out to Mill Creek to do a pre-project site visit, I could not have imagined the amount of trash on the banks of the waterway. There was a debris pile 15 feet high and 150 yards deep," Amy said. "Everything from industrial park waste and pallets packed full of goods to Public Works-issued trash cans and tires were piled up. It was an unbelievable site. The scale was massive."

On June 17, 2010, Amy and Doug's teams guided 200 volunteers on each side of Mill Creek. The work was extremely physical, and the weather was incredibly hot. Still, Doug recalled, "It was a great day for teamwork."

"The debris was so dense we formed assembly lines from the water to the Dumpster," Amy said. "Those lines were 100 people long. There were pieces too big for trash bags, so volunteers would pass the debris from person to person on the assembly line."

Watching Dumpsters fill up and people work together was an incredible sight. "[It was] so great that it was too good to be true," said Doug.

In addition to placing garbage in Dumpsters and separating out hazardous waste, the volunteers also recycled. Pallets, tires and trash cans were pulled aside. Metro Public Works picked up the trash cans, and Bridgestone took the tires. Public, private and nonprofit sectors worked together to accomplish a seemingly impossible task.

This first experience was so positive that three more Mill Creek cleanups followed with diverse volunteer groups ranging from Jack Daniel's employees to Westminster Presbyterian Church members.

Doug said these volunteers – like the thousands of other volunteers he and his staff managed in the past – felt good about the cleanup experience. "But after what we went through in May, the Mill Creek cleanup brought a whole new significance."

Harpeth River Watershed Association & Harpeth River

As a result of the flood, the Harpeth River experienced a record crest in Bellevue resulting in massive debris deposits along its banks.

"Some of the problems we were dealing with were whole buildings were in the river or on its banks," said the Harpeth River Watershed Association's Michael Cain. "Metal was a problem. So were nails. The obvious thing was anyone floating the river was endangered. And there was danger of clogging and flooding even in a smaller rain."

Volunteers did much to improve the Harpeth's condition. "So far we have removed a little more than 80 tons of debris," Michael said about the agency's work in 2010, adding that more than four tons were removed by mid 2011.

Two Harpeth River cleanup projects were completed in partnership with Hands On Nashville in 2010.

"Working in the Harpeth River is different than Mill Creek," said HON's Amy Maloney. "The river's banks are much steeper and the debris is almost entirely personal, since that area is residential. Instead of pallets and Styrofoam, volunteers found children's toys and tool sheds. It was people's treasures we were finding along the banks."

Volunteers again worked in assembly lines. Since the river's banks were steep, volunteers tied themselves to trees, using the trees as anchors. Pulley systems were used to remove debris.

"One of the homeowners we helped lived along Beech Bend," Amy recalled. "Water filled her house to its roofline. Although much of her home's contents were swept away by the water, we were able to return some items, including a family Bible. It was a deeply rewarding experience for the volunteers and everyone involved."

From stabilization to restoration:

VOLUNTEERS REBUILD

By July 2010, Hands On Nashville's work in flood-damaged homes transitioned from stabilization to restoration. A partnership was launched with Rebuilding Together Nashville, and volunteers began helping 50 homeowners revitalize their residences.

Chris Soper, a Lowe's manager in Nashville, stepped forward to lend his knowledge and his hands. He recognized that the need was great, and the scope of work was challenging.

Over three months, Chris recruited 140 volunteers from 11 Lowe's stores to join him, donating their time and skill to the effort. With his leadership, seven homes were completely reconstructed. Chris and his colleagues completed each task, from the installation of new flooring to the refurbishing of kitchen cabinets.

About his experience, Chris said, "Knowing people's lives were completely turned upside down, and that there were neighbors down the street who needed help ... I couldn't help but feel moved to make a difference."

Many others had similar feelings, including Brian Hirst, a customer service manager at Ford Credit. Like Chris, Brian knew he could contribute to the rebuild effort. He organized 100 of his co-workers on four different project sites.

> "Knowing people's lives were completely turned upside down, and that **there were neighbors down the street who needed help** ...I couldn't help but feel moved to make a difference." – *Chris Soper*

By helping people who had need, Brian and his counterparts received much in return. "We were all so touched by the homeowners who we were able to help," he recalled. "It was a privilege for us to assist them."

The homeowners felt the same about the volunteers who entered their homes. "I am thrilled ... beyond thrilled," one homeowner named Nancy said about volunteers' contributions to her home.

The first floor of Nancy's River Plantation condo had four feet of water inside, destroying floors, walls, appliances — everything. Prior to receiving help through this program, she completed some of the needed repairs herself while living on the second floor. With volunteers' leadership, the downstairs of her townhouse was restored the day after her 53rd birthday.

With the generous investments of volunteers' time and talents, as well as hundreds of financial investments from individuals, foundations, corporations and many others, Hands On Nashville's rebuilding program exceeded its 2010 goals. With the Community Foundation of Middle Tennessee and the West Nashville Flood Recovery Network added as partners, restoration projects were completed in 92 houses – 42 more than expected.

- HON's Jaclyn Khoury with Chris Soper.-

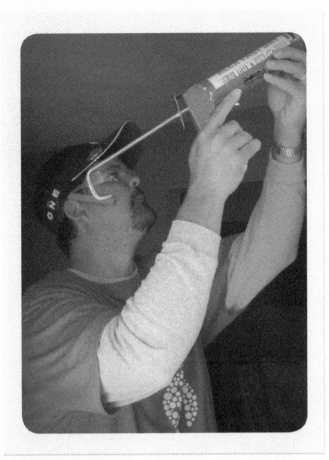

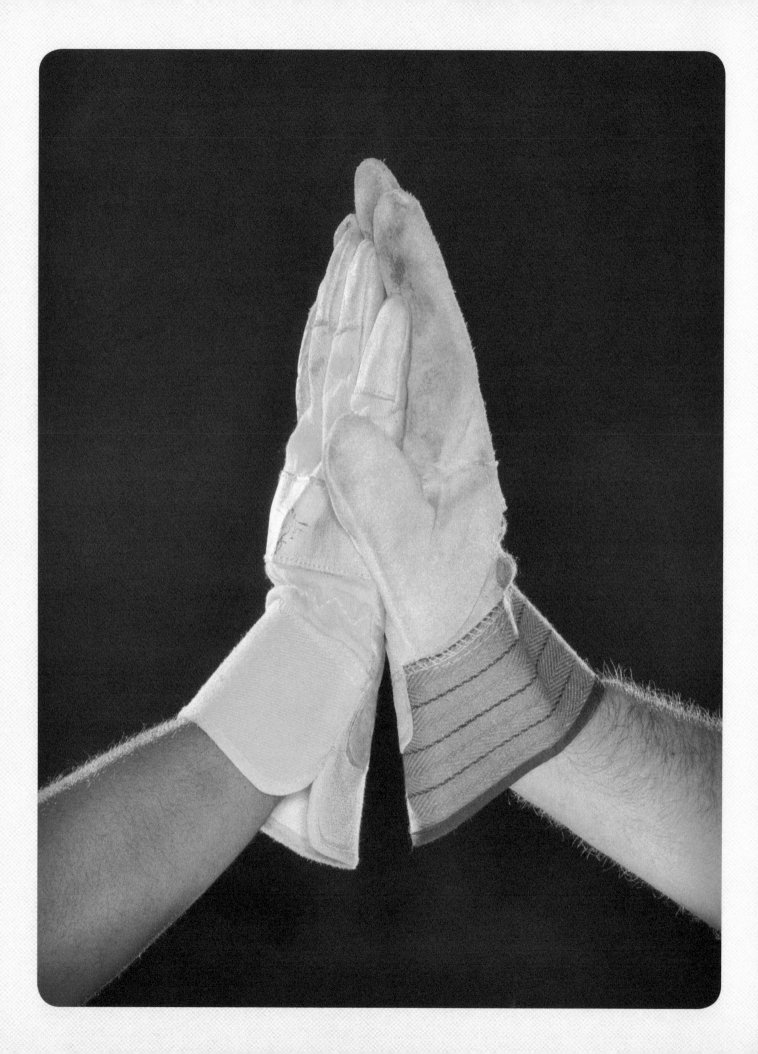

CHURCH ON A MISSION

HOMES & FAMILIES

In years past, the congregation of Westminster Presbyterian Church in Nashville has organized quarterly mission trips to areas in need, such as to the Gulf Coast. As May 2010 approached, members were preparing for a trip to Austell, Ga. When the flood hit Nashville, the congregation knew that its help was needed at home.

Terry Rappuhn is a longtime member of the church who frequently went on its mission trips and is a founder of Nations Ministry Center, an organization under the Presbyterian Church USA which provides education to Nashville refugees. She found herself heading up the church's relief effort for flood victims. As a former hospital system chief financial officer, she had been exposed to the central concepts of crisis management and disaster planning before, but had never experienced disaster of this magnitude on the ground floor.

Immediately after the flood, Terry and a core group of volunteers began meeting in the church's parking lot to pitch in where they could. Their ability to volunteer grew after Westminster connected with Hands On Nashville and learned where to send volunteers, and the effort has evolved into something different about every six weeks since it started. The church quickly became a command center and later created Westminster Presbyterian Disaster Assistance, which worked directly with homeowners referred to it by case management personnel.

Volunteers filtered in from around the country; the church hosted them as their guests, housing them in converted Sunday School rooms on newly constructed bunk beds. The first six months saw the work of almost 600 people translate into 18,000 hours in about 60 homes.

"It was such an overwhelming need. There were so many people who were just devastated. We have resources here at the church, but it really needed champions." – *Terry Rappuhn*

"The volunteers found it to be an incredibly rewarding experience, and it's because of the homeowners," Terry said. "Most of the volunteers got to meet the homeowners during the week. They actually knew the person whose home they were working on and the children whose bedroom they were painting."

Terry described how connected to the homeowners the volunteers felt, even in the short amount of time they spent in Nashville. They usually even hosted a dinner for the homeowners at the church once a week, spending time together away from the work sites and the rebuilding process.

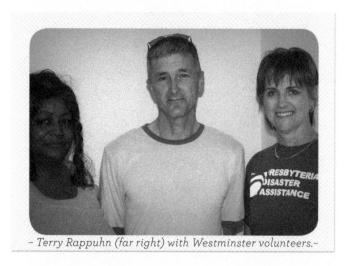

- Terry Rappuhn (far right) with Westminster volunteers. -

In 2011, Terry and the Westminster Disaster Assistance program were able to expand their work through a partnership with Hands On Nashville and two other local faith organizations - West Nashville Flood Recovery Network and Southeast Nashville Recovery. Terry and the leaders of these organizations were able to continue organizing volunteers and coordinating projects through the infrastructure Hands On Nashville provides, allowing them to complete the projects they felt called to do.

Said Brian Rossbert of West Nashville Flood Recovery Network, "The size and scope of the work we have already done together is amazing, and as we look forward, we know we can accomplish even more given the generosity we have already witnessed."

Together, by September 2011, this consortium of three faith organizations and Hands On Nashville was expecting to complete restoration projects in 170

homes referred to them by case managers in all parts of Davidson County. Thanks to the work of people like Terry, Brian, their colleagues at Southeast Nashville Recovery and partners with the other recovery organizations, a corps of volunteers was in place to do this work, coming from around the corner and around the country.

Melissa Thomas of Southeast Nashville Recovery concurred. "How can we not attempt to help every affected homeowner to find healing and a new normal?" she said. "Until the work is done, this is our mission, and it is a mission from God."

"We do it for the homeowners," Terry said. "When I look into their eyes, I can't walk away. It's not about the construction – it's about the people."

NASHVILLE
VOLUNTEER NETWORK

A UNIQUE NATIONAL MODEL

Ken Skalitzky has seen his share of disasters and the responses to them. That's his job.

But in the 13 years that he's been a regional voluntary agency liaison for the Federal Emergency Management Agency, helping coordinate volunteer efforts in the wake of events ranging from Hurricane Katrina to the September 11 terrorist attacks, he had never seen anything quite like what happened in Nashville in May 2010.

Ken said he was especially impressed with the volunteer relief efforts coordinated by Hands On Nashville after the flood.

"The thing that impressed me most was the speed in which the volunteers were activated," Ken said. "The number of volunteers who continued work over the course of the summer was phenomenal and encouraging."

The groundwork for HON's role was laid in 2007 when the organization became a first responder in Metro's Comprehensive Emergency Management Plan. That designation created the distinctive relationship that Hands On Nashville has with Metro government in times of emergency.

In fact, Ken said he is not aware of a similar agreement in any of the other seven Southeastern states he oversees.

Ken was so impressed with the partnership that he highlighted it as part of a "best practices" presentation he gave at the National Conference on Volunteering and Service, which took place in June 2010 in New York City. Nashville Mayor Karl Dean was asked by New York City Mayor Michael Bloomberg to be on hand for that presentation.

"I'd like to see other cities replicate that type of partnership," he said.

Stationed in Nashville from May until September of 2010, Ken also did his part to encourage and sustain volunteerism. He helped develop 17 long-term recovery committees that continue to support flood victims. He hopes all of the volunteers who assisted in the aftermath of the flood will continue to be engaged as well.

"Tennessee is known as the Volunteer State, and that comes with certain expectations," Ken said. "Middle Tennessee's volunteers lived up to that expectation."

> "This is a unique situation. We have not had an event where the volunteer network has been the designated point of contact with the city like it is here. This is a great partnership." – *Ken Skalitzky*

Hands On Nashville extends a special thank you to our friends at the Hard Rock Cafe, SouthComm and CAA for helping us release "Take My Hand" in style on May 2, 2011.

Lightning Source, an Ingram Content Group company, is the leader in providing on-demand print and distribution services for books. Hands On Nashville is fortunate that "Take My Hand" is among those books beginning in May of 2011 – the one-year anniversary of Middle Tennessee's historic flood. Thanks to the Ingram Content Group and the Lightning Source team for enabling Hands On Nashville to print and distribute this important collection of volunteers' triumphs in the wake of disaster.

THANK YOU

MP&F
McNeely Pigott & Fox
Public Relations, LLC

McNeely Pigott & Fox Public Relations is one of the largest independent public relations firms in the Southeast. Hands On Nashville has been an MP&F pro bono client for five years, and the firm has been a significant partner in HON's flood relief communications, including the production of "Take My Hand." McNeely Pigott & Fox staff members wrote and edited this book's stories. In doing so, they interviewed dozens of volunteers. Thanks to Mike Pigott, his partners and every member of the firm whose words tell how Nashville responded to disaster with dignity, courage and generosity.

THE BUNTIN GROUP
BRAND FLUENCY

The Buntin Group is the largest brand communications agency in Tennessee and among the top 100 advertising agencies in the country. But large doesn't mean uncaring. In fact, just the opposite. Buntin is a longtime friend of Hands On Nashville. Over the past eight years, The Buntin Group has participated with HON in the community's biggest day of service in Metro Nashville Public Schools, Hands On Nashville Day. This year they stepped up to do even more. The Buntin Group generously agreed to design this beautiful book, "Take My Hand." To the Buntin family and the entire Buntin team, thank you for artfully portraying a Nashville that's united in service. Your contributions to "Take My Hand" are proof that Nashville is truly a city of volunteers.

CPSIA information can be obtained
at www.ICGtesting.com
225068LV00001BA

* 9 7 8 0 6 1 5 4 5 2 2 4 1 *